Floating For Two

Floating For Two

Brian Hronek

iUniverse, Inc.
New York Lincoln Shanghai

Floating For Two

iUniverse, Inc.

For information address:
iUniverse, Inc.
2021 Pine Lake Road, Suite 100
Lincoln, NE 68512
www.iuniverse.com

For Patent information on Floating for Two, contact the U.S. Patent and Trademark Office.

ISBN: 0-595-32432-0

Printed in the United States of America

To Stephanie, Jacob, and Jonah & Nicholas: For you are the inspiration that keeps me afloat, during the rough seas of life!

Contents

Preface

Everyone has dreams and aspirations about their lives, what paths they will follow, into and throughout adulthood. For many, those dreams fade into the backdrop of reality, nothing more than a painting on a wall, hung up or put away for an occasional glance and wonderment, or a dream that vanishes of detail other than it's memory.

Those willing to look deep into their hearts to find that one force by which they can be successful are not just the objects in the paintings but those holding the brush. Just like the artist who knows that he must continue to improve on his work, searching for new and improved ways to enlighten his audience, we too must continue our search, finding new and inventive ways to reach our goals and full-fill our lives.

Never forget that without supporting and loving those most precious in your life, you are no better than that painting in the closet, fading away into a blank canvas or the vivid details of a dream that vanish with time.

This book does not contain the words written by a man of science, psychology or philosophy, just the experiences and struggles of one ordinary person like many of us, searching for his dreams, his hopes and his ideas for the perfect life.

Is this a true story? It's meaning will be different for everyone, each reader must face his or her own dreams and paint his or her own picture, overcoming the struggles in life that lead us to the place we so desire.

The Agony of Defeat

1

Sitting in my office, behind my oak trimmed desk. I look out of the window and watch the water spilling from the fountain that adorns the gardens, just east of the building. I cannot help but to think how fortunate I am. The perfect career, family and all of the material wants a person can afford. Tapping my pen against my lips I remember how I made it this far and I never forgot the inspiration that helped me discover my dreams.

While taking a few moments to glance out at the beautiful scenery, I notice several of my employees arriving for work. I begin to smile, I am happy with the hard work and dedication they have shown to launch my product and business off the ground and into market. As I continue watching, I notice Shaun walking through the lot, talking on his cell phone. He is not just a great friend but the best damn partner a person can hope to employ.

As I become lost in my own world of deep thought, my office telephone rings. Turning in my chair, I casually pick up the line and answer, "This is Steve." "Steve, your wife is on the line, would you care to speak with her?" The voice on the other line reports, not just any voice but it is the person behind the voice. "Yes, I will take the call," I respond. "I'll send her through and don't forget you have an interview at ten o'clock this morning," Vickie says as she transfers Amy's call to my office.

"Hi Amy, is everything all right?" I answer, looking at the family photo that sits upon my desk as I wait for Amy to respond. "Are you coming home for dinner tonight or will you be working late, again?"

Amy says with a hint of frustration in her voice. "Sweetheart, once I get the production numbers from my sales team I will be right home, probably no later than six. And by the way it's only ten minutes until eight, why ask me that question now?" We chat for a few moments and then we say our goodbyes.

As the morning hours pass, my line rings once again. I look down and see that it is Vickie, my office manager. "Yes, Vickie," I say pausing for her to respond. "Your ten o'clock is here, should I send them in?" "Give me about five minutes, and shove them through," I reply in a jovial tone.

Waiting for the entrance of my appointment, I clean my desk trying to look as organized as possible. I may be the president of the company but even I should not be without dignity and class.

A few moments later, the door opens and in walks my appointment. A tall well-dressed woman, presented as if she were going to work on Wall Street, enters the room and approaches my desk.

"Please have a seat," I say as I make my way from behind my desk to greet her. She shakes my hand and introduces herself to me as Olivia. "So, Olivia you are here for…" I could not remember, "Why was she here?" I recall Vickie telling me that I had an interview at ten o'clock but I was not hiring anyone at this time.

Beads of sweat begin to develop on my brow, I cannot possibly refuse this woman the time. After all, she went out of her way to seek a new career and apparently liked what she saw regarding my company.

Just as I was about to explain my situation, she pulls out a notebook and begins to speak. "First, I would like to thank you for taking time from your busy schedule to speak with me about your company and your motivation for starting this project."

I sit up in my chair and begin to listen intently. I look at her and stare, confused for just a moment as she continues to explain.

"I am writing a paper on small business development, a requirement for a course at the University and you had sent me a letter with a day and time that we could meet."

As she says those words, I suddenly remember. "Oh, yes, I do remember!" I exclaim as I realize the purpose of her visit. She looks at me with squinting eyebrows as she too realizes that I had not known the purpose for her visit, until this very moment.

"I'm terribly sorry, Olivia," I say as I lean back in my leather chair, rocking back and forth. She smiles and nods her head showing me that my apology has been accepted. "If you don't mind I would like to ask you a few questions about your company and the motivation that has made you such a success in your industry," Olivia says while writing on her notepad.

I stand up and walk from behind the desk, over to a small bar that I had placed in the office. Nothing too fancy, just a place to hold cold beverages for visiting guests. I grab two bottles of water and walk back to her direction. "Here you go, just in case you get thirsty, I have soft drinks or juice if you prefer," I say offering a gesture of gratitude and an apology for the miss communication of her visit. "Thank you Mr. Woods, water is fine," Olivia says taking the water from my hand.

I make my way back to my seat, put my elbows on the desktop and begin to give Olivia my full attention.

"What would you like to ask me?" I say, enthused about giving her any helpful information regarding the success of my company.

"I have done research on your company so I am familiar with the products that you manufacture, however, I would like you to tell me the motivation for developing this company, your products."

"Wow!" I think to myself, the motivation for my products, nevertheless, how do I tell her the inspiration for my success in just a few sentences? I begin to wonder, "How much time she has, how fast can she write?" "Absolutely," I reply trying to recall the events that have led up to this particular time in my life.

"First, let me make a quick phone call." I pick up the phone and dial Vickie's line. "Hold all of my calls until further notice. I will be in an important meeting." As I say those words, I look at Olivia with a smile on my face and give her an approving nod. She smiles back knowing that I will be giving her my full attention. I hang up the phone and sit back comfortably in my chair. "Let me see where do I begin?" I think to myself.

"Olivia, I'm going to tell you a story about this company, our product, however, in order for you to grasp the concept for its foundation, I will have to start at the beginning, the beginning of this company, the beginning of my life. You see I was alone, confused and…" Remembering a time, not too distant in my past, I continue.

Twirling my glass on its edge, I glance out Nancy's window and see the most beautiful sunset ever. I am as comfortable as I can be in a place I know I should not be, when my cell phone rings.

"Hello," I answer, mustering up the energy to sound as if everything in the world is as it should be. "When are you coming home? I have something important to tell you, Lover." Lover, the pet name my wife has used to get my attention since we began dating. "Honey, as soon as I finish up at the office," I reply with a cheerful, yet hidden fear of what she will say if, somehow she knows that I am not at the office.

I wonder what she has to tell me, could it be something my sons have done in school or maybe a letter she has received from her mother. I hurry along our conversation and we say our goodbyes.

Just as I start to embrace wild thoughts about the bit of news that awaits my return home, I notice my friend Shaun sitting at a table with some of his business colleagues. He is ordering drinks and shuffling through papers on the table. "Shit, I never come to Nancy's alone, no one does. How do I explain this to Shaun?" If I should be so lucky that he glances my way, I think to myself hoping to leave unnoticed.

I set my glass down on the bar and in a stealthy manner make my way to the door, a few more steps and I am out. I am free, free from any explanations or excuses about my presence. I lean against the wall just outside the bar and stare blankly into the dawn, thinking of ways to tell my family about the day's turn of events. I think of ways to tell my sons who have always looked up to me as their provider, coach, teacher and most importantly hero. In addition, Amy, what do I tell Amy? "Wait," I whisper to myself as I regain my composure. I need to get home; to my kids, my wife and most importantly to the news that awaits my return.

Feeling a little more confident about giving Shaun the slip from the bar and feeling anticipation for the news at home, I reach into my coat pocket for my keys, and nothing. "What did I do with my keys?" I mutter aloud to myself, searching through every pocket I possess. "What-ever," I say to myself as I lay my head on top of the car remembering that I had taken them out of my pocket when paying the tab.

I slowly make my way back into Nancy's and as fate would have it, Shaun looks up from the table and peers at me through his tiny spectacles. "Steven!" He howls my name as if we had just met after years of absence from each other's company. "Hi Shaun," I reply with a nod of the head and a short wave.

Shaun stands from his seat and attempts to introduce me to his company. Shaking hands and using my most professional voice, I take note of each individual's name yet, trying not to make eye contact. Even though I am dressed in similar attire, I cannot help but feel inferior to the party before me. During the brief conversation, I glance at the bar and see the shimmering glow from the keys that have sealed my fate.

After glancing over at the bar and then focusing my attention to the group, Shaun gives me the low eyebrow look as if he is asking me why I am at Nancy's. "Well, I have to run, Shaun I'll call you later." As I say those words, I walk over to the bar, grab my keys, and quickly make my exit through the door, once again.

Even though Shaun had seen me at Nancy's, I feel as if I had escaped with what little dignity I had left. I begin to make the journey home, I cannot help but think how my life will change, how our lives will change. Wondering, pondering about the plans my wife and I have made for our future and how those plans and dreams were squashed with one swipe of the pen. A decision made by a group of individuals

that live and die by the bottom line. Oh, yes, earlier today I was eliminated, downsized and expelled, from not just a job but also a career.

This was a position that I have worked to develop since my gradua-
tion from the University. A position that allowed me to think for
myself, using my creativity in ways not many organizations will allow
one man to achieve throughout his or her career. As an International
Trade Consultant, I was responsible for many of the products that
arrived in the United States from manufacturers around the world.
Products to be sold by retail outlets and warehoused in large distribution networks but now, I am alone to fend for myself, without the
security of a paycheck or the stability of having a purpose each day. It
seems almost unreal, like a bad dream but I remain focused knowing
that my skills and experiences will allow me to find another position
with a stable company.

I pull into the driveway of my home not much more than a mile
from Nancy's bar and grill. As I get out of my car, the two reasons I get
up every morning come racing out the front door. "Last one to hug
dad is a rotten egg!" My oldest son of eight yells to his younger brother
of five.

I bend down to hug my sons, and as always, I have to give the five
year old his dues. As I am bending down hugging my sons, I glance up
and see my beautiful wife standing in the doorway of our home. Her
long blond hair and her smooth silky skin always remind me of the day
we first met and how fortunate I am to be married to such an amazing
woman. I stand giving the boys a pat on the head and begin to make
my way to the front porch.

"Hello," I say to my wife as I give her a small kiss on the mouth, trying to act as if everything is as it should be. I also notice that she has a
tear in her eye and yet a small smile eluding from her lips. "Come
inside there is something I have to tell you," she replies while taking me
by the hand.

Again, I start to think about the news she has to tell me and by the
look on her face; I am not sure what to think. "Honey, you know I

don't like surprises, just tell me if someone has died," I say with a crackle in my voice. "Why do you always assume the worst Steven?" she replies frustrated that I am spoiling this moment.

As I stare at her glowing face I think to myself, what good news can there possibly be after the days events at the office. Amy begins to fidget with my shirt collar and looking straight into my eyes she begins to speak. "Do you remember when we talked about having another baby and how hard we have been trying for the past few months?"

"How could I forget, Amy? Trying has been the best part, however; I am not really in the mood right now. Something happened at work today and I need some time to think about how to handle the situation," I respond while moving slightly away from Amy's touching fingers. "I'm sorry Lover but, I think what I'm about to say will make your day much brighter," Amy says while glancing at the chair beside me.

I sit down at the kitchen table awaiting the news. "Close your eyes and don't peek," she instructs in a most exciting voice. "Okay but…" Before I can finish, Amy puts her finger to my lips and draws an imaginary line from them down to the base of my chin, as a seductive sign to listen. She tells me to stand up and guides me into the next room. It is obvious that she wants to cheer me up but I am not sure that sex is going to work this time.

Nevertheless, I cannot let her down after she has worked so hard to make this moment romantic, is this what she has done? The boys playing in the front yard, what will they see if they walk into the house? It is not time for lovemaking.

While starring at the back of my eyelids I ask, "The news, what about the news you are anxious to tell me?" "Okay, open your eyes," she says in a quiet and seductive voice. I slowly open my eyes, not to find her in a soft teddy or, even half-naked but, instead holding a long white applicator not two inches from my face.

"Congratulations daddy, we're pregnant!" The excitement getting the better of her as she screams, jumping into my arms as if to tackle me in pure excitement and joy. "That's great Honey," I say jumping up and down while she holds on for dear life.

"We're also unemployed!" The words bursting from my lips followed seconds later with an eerie silence. The jumping and screaming comes to a sudden halt and I lower Amy to the floor, onto her feet.

"What do you mean you're unemployed?" Amy asks, backing away from me, eagerly waiting for my response. I explain to her about the meeting at work today. How the board of directors felt that in order to maintain a competitive edge in the market they would have to cut costs.

"...and that's the way it happened, our entire department was eliminated. Not just here but across the country." I add removing my tie and thumbing through the day's mail left on the table. "Couldn't they offer you another position or something?" Amy asks still in denial that my last day of work was effective immediately. "That's not how it works, they make a decision to fatten their wallets and we have to live with those choices." Nothing I can say or do at this time will help explain or comfort my wife nor, am I in the mood to relive the day's events a second time.

The evening ahead is a sobering occasion, nothing said at dinner accept the occasional questions and thoughts that all young children have while engaging in social events with their parents. Our sons knew that not all was right in the Wood's house, after all, they grow up so fast that most of the time we forget that they are capable of listening and comprehending our conversations.

Usually after dinner, my wife and I spend the evenings talking of the day's events, watching television and playing with our sons, however, this night produced an atmosphere of quietness and tension making way for the development of depression and despair that will fill the next few months of our lives.

That night while preparing for bed my wife and I spoke, not just for the first time since we both shared our news but also, at the same time.

"Honey, lover," we both say while looking down at the bed covers, each of us waiting for the other to respond. During the short pause, I take the liberty of speaking first. "I think it's great that we are going to have another baby, even with what happened at the office that is the best news I've heard since the conception of our first two children."

After revealing those words, I slowly look up at my wife to show her that I meant what I had said, and I knew what I had to do to support my family, financially. "We will make it happen, we always pull through," I say making my way around the bed and kissing her gently on the forehead, excusing myself from the room.

As I retire to my den those words I spoke to Amy in our bedroom begin to fog my mind keeping me from the task of seeking employment. "How did I know that we would be all right?" This unemployment situation was a first for me, for us. I sit in my leather office chair and turn on the computer, waiting for the system to adjust. I look around my office and stare at the awards and recognitions that adorn the walls of my sanctuary, reflecting on these awards and the feelings I had for reaching those achievements.

I can remember standing in front of the Board of Directors giving an acceptance speech for an award very few employees have had the privilege to earn. I knew that receiving this award would guarantee my status within the company and praise among my colleagues.

I begin to drift into the past placing myself in the very situation that left me feeling confident and strong, not just about myself but my career. I remember driving to the banquet laughing and conversing with Amy, feeling as if I were on top of the world. Amy's eyes filling with pride and she portrays an attitude that she is honored to be my wife. During the ceremony, the president of the company presents me with a plaque, which recognizes the changes, and developments I have made within the organization and department.

Feelings of frustration and rage begin to set in as my thoughts return to the present. Once again, I begin focusing on finding a new career, trying to put the selfishness of a company behind me.

Typing on the keyboard, searching for web sites that promote available positions I become worried about finding work. It has been twelve years since I looked for a job and just as long since I have interviewed for a position. "What will I say to a potential employer? Will I be qualified to work for them?" These thoughts keep racing through my mind blocking any concentration for finding work.

Gazing at the computer, I cannot help but think about the worst-case scenarios that lie before me. Is it the glare of the computer screen in the dim light of my office? Can it be the ticking of the clock? What ever it is, I am mesmerized in thought and it is not about finding the moneymaker, that golden career that lies in wait. I cannot stop thinking about the future of our financial situation, "Will we become wards of the state? Will I end up like so many others that have lost everything; their house, cars and sanity?" Again, more questions surfacing within my mind.

I begin to doze off in my chair, one hand on the mouse and the other hand under my chin, as if in deep thought. The longer I sit in my chair, the deeper and deeper I fall into slumber. A few times jumping as if someone has startled me but, then quickly falling back to sleep.

2

I begin to dream of soft white beaches, a grass hut, my wife and I walking along the shore hand in hand as the water gently cascades over our feet and back again. We are laughing and talking yet, the words are unknown to me in my sleep. As we continue our walk, I see a pier extending out towards the sea.

A long wooden platform used by fishermen and the occasional tourist walking among its wooden planks. As we continue our journey I realize that it is no ordinary pier but, a place filled with tables, well-dressed individuals and a fully stocked bar with signs of my companies logo, or should I say, "My ex-company." The signs are carefully hanging about as if they were sponsoring a trade show of sorts.

I notice a large round table on the wooden platform centered amongst the others, which are entertaining many enthusiastic guests yet, faceless in my dream. I notice that sitting at the large center table are the board of directors and the department manager, Gabe Williams, the one crowned with the honors of delivering me the termination letter.

As my wife and I approach the pier, I can make out some arguing and negotiating from the center table as if someone were justifying a thought or an action. I continue walking, picking up my pace, nervous that I may miss some important news or, maybe anxious that they will ask me to return to work tomorrow. As I draw closer, I can hear voices calling my name, "Steve, come join us!" I make my way to the table and reply, "I hope you don't mind if I bring my wife."

They look at each other with puzzling eyes, and at that moment, I realize my wife is absent from my presence, nowhere to be found. "Could I have lost her while rushing to get to the pier? Did I lose her in the crowd?" While looking around anxiously, I notice someone taking me by the hand. I try to identify the mysterious face while being led to a seat reserved for me, a seat at the head of the table. The faceless escort introduces me to the executives who are staring at me as if they have been expecting me all along and by the looks on their faces; it seems as if they are waiting for me to say something profound or inventive.

"Steve, sit have a drink," Gabe says starring at me with conflicting eyes. As I sit down and prepare to join in the conversation, I quickly realize that the discussions seem to be not with me but about me, or, my mind would have me believe. I continue looking back and forth around the table that was once so inviting, trying to understand my surroundings, trying to make eye contact with the familiar yet unknowing faces before me.

The confusion distracts me from my immediate company and I notice others in the background, sipping wine and other spirits, slightly speaking amongst one another through the sounds of tropical music floating effortlessly in the breeze.

After a few moments of nervously searching for answers to questions I have not asked, I strain to make out the voices before me only to hear phrases such as, "Steve, we did it for your own good," and, "let him be the inventor of his own fate."

"What did this mean?" So many questions and yet, no one showed any consideration for explanation. I begin shouting in the hopes of drawing attention to myself but my words fall on deaf ears. Suddenly, I feel a cold wet glass touching my fingertips as the waiter sets a drink upon the table. I look up at the man hoping that he will provide some sense of normalcy to the strange surroundings.

I open my eyes and to my surprise, the family dog is pushing on my hand with her cold wet nose. "Was I dreaming? Did the dream have any purpose?" I think to myself then quickly pass the dream off as a stressful passing of the day's events and realizing that it is two-thirty in the morning. I pat the dog on the head and turn off the computer, wearily dragging myself to bed and for a short time lying there hoping that this day too, was just a bad dream.

3

Days go by without any word from companies responding to the hundreds of resumes that I have submitted over the internet and through the mail. The days pass into weeks and by now I am beginning to show my desperation. I have not shaved in days and it seems that I have worn the same shirt and pants for the past two weeks. I have lost my purpose, a reason to get out of bed every morning.

I cannot understand why there are no job offers before me and yet, I know the reasons. This is a time of corporate greed, saving money and cutting expenses. My previous salary and the possibility of paying relocation costs were most likely not in my favor when being considered by potential employers. After all, someone at my ex-company was doing my job, someone lucky enough to take on multiple responsibilities with less pay. The economic world is changing and I have not prepared for the challenges that lie ahead.

I wonder around the house without purpose, without stability, waking from sleep in the same cloths I had worn to bed the night before. The only energies that I can call upon are the thoughts and questions that haunt my every waking moment. In the depths of my mind, I realize that the money from my severance package is running thin and our savings will soon be lost yet, I cannot bring myself to seek employment that offers low wages and little satisfaction. I continue to hold onto the belief that there is a company somewhere, interested in my resume.

I journey to my den as I often do each day, mostly looking for work but often just passing the time away keeping my hand on the mouse as if waiting for the computer to tell me I have mail or a possible response from my resumes. Sitting in my den planning my next move, I hear my wife rummaging about in the kitchen. "Honey, I'm going to the grocery. Is there anything you would like?" Amy asks, while scurrying about looking for her purse and keys. "How about a job," I think quietly to myself. "Nothing special dear, be careful," I reply with as much enthusiasm as I can produce.

She walks by the den and sticks her head through the door. "Don't forget about the Unemployment Office this afternoon," she says in a stern and demanding tone. I continue starring at the computer screen as if I am alone, no response forming on my tongue. Maybe it was the tone of her spoken words or the reality of my situation but I lost all control. Not out in the open for Amy to view rather, in my head. In my mind, I can hear the snapping of twigs from my sanity tree. Branches falling to the earth and smashing into the ground and with every word Amy speaks another branch is falling. I cannot take much more, not from Amy, nor, any negative situation that will befall me. I continue sitting in silence uttering not a word from my lips as I stare at the computer screen watching her reflection disappear from the doorway of my den.

Amy pulls out of the driveway to begin her alone time at the grocery and I walk from the den upstairs to the bedroom to clean up for my visit to the Unemployment Office, pulling out my suit from the closet and hanging it above the door as I have done so many times in the past.

On the way to the Unemployment Office, I glance in the rear view mirror and look at myself, noticing my clean-shaven face and neatly combed hair. Ironically, I begin to feel better about myself, no longer upset at Amy or the situation, that has swallowed me these past few weeks.

This was the first time I have worn a suit since the lay offs and it felt good, it felt right. As I pull into the parking lot I notice others drifting in and out of the office doors, only there were no other suites and ties to be found. I sit in my car for a few moments watching people enter the building mostly dressed in casual attire and a few as if they had just climbed out of bed.

My feelings of confidence begin to exit my body as I take off my jacket and remove my tie. It is now that I realize I no longer hold the title of International Trade Consultant but that of unemployed, a statistic for the media. I make my way into the office, a place unfamiliar to my sights and notice a line as long as those of an amusement park ride.

I take my place in the procession and look forward, down at the ground hoping that no one notices me or will remember my face, if we should by chance meet again.

As the line snakes through the office, I can over hear individuals conversing among one another, their personalities as jovial and complacent as one could be in these surroundings. "I'm sure glad I lost my job, it's too hot to work." I hear one voice say as he converses with the man behind him. "I know what you mean, its better on unemployment. No child support," the other man replies as they continue their conversation.

I cannot believe my ears, these two adults discussing the relief they have for not being able to find work. "Where is the work ethic? Are people really this lazy?" I think to myself looking around the room, judging those among my presence, wondering if they too are here looking for an easy escape from responsibility. I am uncomfortable and the longer I stand in line the more depressed and out of place I begin to feel.

I finally reach the desk, handing the woman my paper work and identification. As she fumbles through her computer keys, she begins asking questions about my past employment and the reason for my termination. Her choice of words and the tone of her voice create feelings of disgust and outrage within me. "Miss, I was not terminated. I was let go due to economic situations…." Before I can finish my explanation, she looks up at me from behind the desk and replies, "I understand sir but, the computer program only gives us a few choices and termination is the closest match."

She hands me some printed forms and advises me that I can complete them online, at home. Finally, some reprieve and I will not have to attend another line session with individuals that want to be a number in a system that seems all too liberal.

As I gather my belongings and walk towards the door, I notice a man standing in line dressed in a similar suit, waiting his turn to file for unemployment benefits. Not far behind him is a woman with four children, standing silent looking at the floor in front of her while maintaining watch of her brood. I continue from the office and begin to feel a little guilty of the prejudice thoughts I have regarding those in line, others in my similar situation hoping to find some financial relief. Still it was hard, being somewhere, a place you know in your mind and feel in your heart you do not belong.

On the drive home, I think deeply about my relationship with Amy and the kids, fighting and bickering about everything, on every occasion. It has not been easy trying to be the perfect family man and yet, there has to be a purpose to my existence. If this was a test from God, I was about to fail.

The more my wondering mind projects pictures of my family, the more content I seem to be, even breaking a smile on my weathered face. Even though I have lost what I thought to be the best damn job in the world, when I was in the presence of my children, I illuminated a glow as if nothing seemed to matter. Sometimes, I even out glow my wife and she is three months pregnant, go figure.

I pull into the driveway noticing Amy has not returned from the grocery. I am not sure how long I have been away but still I am a little worried about her safety. I walk inside our home and put on a clean pair of shorts and shirt, preparing myself for the antagonizing questions Amy will have about my trip to the Unemployment Office.

I return downstairs and make my way to the living room to relax and take my mind off my problems with a little afternoon television.

Not long after retiring to the couch the telephone rings, not just your everyday ring but THE RING, the one that a person anticipates for days or even longer, while waiting for some type of news. I stare from the living room across the way to where the telephone waits in its secretive yet, all knowing cradle.

As I approach the telephone to answer, I cannot help but pray that this is the call that will rescue my family from sure and certain financial agony. "Hello," I answer with an uncertainty in my voice. "Yes, is this Mr. Woods?" The professional and confident voice on the other end replies. "Yes, yes it is," I answer with the confidence that a mouse has, finding crumbs on the floor yet, unsure why it is attached to a piece of wood with a metal bar. "This is Mr. Kelly from Welgo..."

Before he can finish I lose all control of my manners and in an excited voice, I break into his sentence and reply, "Are you calling in response to a resume that I sent earlier this month?" There was a short pause. "Not exactly sir," the man says with a confused tone in his voice. "I'm calling on behalf of your car loan and you seem to be a month behind."

I can only compare my reaction to those few spoken words from the voice on the other line to that of a horse race, that is right, a horse race. You know the one where the losing horse comes from behind and the leading jockey looks over his shoulder with that, oh shit look in his eyes. Well, I was not that come from behind horse; this is a telephone call that I am not prepared to handle. I have never been late on payments for anything, how was I going to handle these situations? What do I tell the voice on the other end of the phone? Yet, for a split second, I desperately wonder if they have any openings at their company.

I put the phone back to my ear and explain my situation; I know that I have to discuss this with Amy, nevertheless, how do I play the role of intermediary between my wife, whom handles the finances, and our many creditors who will only speak to the person with the name on the accounts? It looks like I am in for a lesson in the art of personal finances.

After our conversation, I feel as if I am a bad man, a man that is not responsible, incapable of managing his own life. Who ever that person was that just called, had taken pride in knocking me down a few more steps from my self-esteem ladder. Another day in paradise, I think to myself and just like that, it seems that there is no hope for a new career.

Speaking of paradise, I sit down on the couch and begin to engage in a program on the television but I cannot forget about my dream a few nights past. The company that decided to ruin my life was it also going to ruin my sanity and corrupt my family's dreams.

Oh well, I never believed in the interpretation of dreams and I am not about to start now, after all, where are the beautiful swimsuit models that I have dreamt about in the past? When my wife dreams, would she be married to me if dreams came true? Would Amy ride off into the sunset with her fantasized night and shinning armor upon a white steed, leaving me to rot in self-pity and shame? "What ever," I say to myself. These thoughts in my head seem so preposterous and yet, I find the ideas reoccurring in my mind.

I return to the television with remote in hand. "Okay, hear we go," I say aloud while flipping through the channels. The wife is shopping the kids are in school and I am all alone. "Do I dare open a beer on a weekday, in the afternoon?" As I continue my journey through the numerous channels of deceit and corruption, the telephone rings. Once again, I slowly make my way to the cradle of distrust and pick up the receiver. I hold the telephone away from my ear close enough to hear but, far enough away as if I do not want to know whose calling.

If you have ever watched a scary movie and held your hand over your eyes but spread your fingers so you can still see what is happening, those are my feelings.

"Hello, may I speak with Mr. Woods?" The voice on the other end responds. "I know, I know, I owe you money but, you will have to wait until my wife returns home from the grocery before I give you any information on our financial situation. I lost my job and…" The mysterious voice on the other end quickly interrupts, "Oh no Mr. Woods,

I'm calling in response to a resume that you had submitted earlier this month and we would like to set up an interview with you later this week."

I cannot believe my ears, a response, however, I am not sure if I am elated with joy that I could possibly be working again or, that I had just made a huge ass out of myself assuming the call was from a bill collector.

"No time to worry now," I quickly think to myself as I continue with the most educated excuse for justifying my previous words. "I'm sorry, I thought you were a telemarketer wanting me to purchase something nice for my home or, refinance for the tenth time this month."

"What a recovery," I thought. Did the mysterious voice on the other end buy my excuse? "I would love to set up an interview," I quickly continue. "Great, how about Friday at nine o'clock, and here are the directions..." I write as fast as the voice on the other end can speak and then thank him for the opportunity. After hanging up the telephone, I look back over the notes that I had just scribbled down on paper.

I am so overjoyed that I look up to the ceiling, raise my hands into the air and yell, "Holy Shit!" I have forgotten the name of the company and what position I would be interviewing. "Not a problem," I think to myself. I will call back and when they answer, I will take note of the company name and hang up.

I start to thumb through the numbers on the caller identification, OUT OF AREA; the name reads on the telephone. "Come on, give me a break," I grumble aloud. "At least I have an address, a time and place, that will have to do for now," I continue thinking.

Elated from the news I stroll to my den and begin to prepare for Friday's meeting, anticipating Amy's return home. Not long after, I notice from the window in my den, Amy pulling into the driveway or, attempting to back into the driveway as she does so many times when arriving home from a much-anticipated trip to the grocery. "Hurry, let's get the food inside before the kids get home," I say rushing to the car offering my assistance. We begin pulling bags from the trunk of the car, carrying as many of them as our strength will allow.

You see, whenever my wife comes home from the store, our kitchen becomes an arena for taste testing. It seems that every bag and box are torn into for just a smidgen of a taste and then left for dead or, until mom cleans up the mess.

We hurry in with the bags of food and in a joint effort; I assist in stashing the goods but only for a moment. Soon the kids will be home and interrogating the poor boxes of cookies and other snacks that are so neatly packaged for our enjoyment.

"I have a bit of good news honey," I boast as if I am a shy schoolgirl asking for that first kiss. "Did you get a job?" Amy asks while shifting her head out from the pantry to look my way. "No, not exactly, however, I do have an interview for Friday and it sounds promising. Oh, and by the way it is not just a job, remember I think I am still a professional. Therefore, I would like to think of it as a new career," I respond tossing her a bag of potato chips. "What's the name of the company? What is the position?" Amy asks, not allowing me to get a word in edge wise. "Well the interview is Friday, in the morning and the rest is a secret."

How could I possibly tell her that I was not sure with whom or what the position was before me? I was afraid, not because I was keeping the information a secret but I did not know the answer myself. How could I ever live down my boasting of being a professional, if I was not responsible enough to write down the important details of a telephone call?

"By the way, how are you feeling?" I ask trying desperately to change the subject. "Steve, I don't understand you. Everything is fine one minute and the next you are a complete Ass. I wish you would make up your mind before I lose mine." The tone in her voice was bone chilling. Nothing warm or heartfelt but, more like an observation from an outsider. I was pushing her away and then bringing her back for more agony. I did not respond to her comment and only watch as she puts away the groceries concerned that our marriage may be heading into undiscovered waters.

"Anyhow, I feel great and don't keep secrets from me; I don't think we can handle too many more of those in this house," she continues with a slight chuckle in her voice. "Do I dare ask if you went to the Unemployment Office while I was gone?" She had finally asked the question that had engulfed her every thought while shopping. I quickly respond, "Yes, and it was a nightmare. Do you realize that there are people filing for those benefits that do not intend to go back to work? I am officially a number with the state, a statistic..." Before I can finish Amy replies, "Steve, I don't care about those other people and neither should you, we can use the extra money so quit complaining."

Immediately I knew that I was alone, without the help and support from my spouse, my so-called partner. It almost seems as if every time Amy opens her mouth, the more resentment I feel towards her. It is not her fault or mine that I am out of work, but her bossy ways and intrusive tone seems to push me away.

A few moments of unspoken words pass and we hear the approaching sounds of the school bus. Amy and I look at each other and frantically put what is left of the groceries into the pantry. "I'll finish with the groceries, go see that the kids get in the house safely," Amy says as she relentlessly works to find spare room for the remaining few items.

I step outside and wait for the arrival of my shinning stars, it is spring and the weather is just cool enough outside to welcome the return of summer. The bus pulls up and without a skip in time I hear that golden word, "Daddy, daddy!" My sons yell as they step off the bus and race in my direction. I have not had many opportunities while I was working to be home, waiting for them in the afternoon to greet them from a long day of school. I bend down to give my kisses and hugs, the five year old of course, bringing up the rear.

"Last but not least," I shout as he tackles me in the front yard. While lying on my back in the grass I look at my sons and say, "Listen very carefully boys, mom went to the store..." Before I am able to finish my sentence, they are sprinting towards the house and into the kitchen.

As I get up from the lawn and brush my clothes, I shake my head, for I know the events that will soon be taking place. Oh, the rape and pillaging that is about to happen on those poor, unsuspecting treats is an event that only a mother can love and of course manage.

I walk into the house, sneak into my den and quietly shut the door, a person can only take so many "stop that's" and "don't do that's" in one day. I think I will let mom handle this business and I will sit in the chair that has been home to me for the last few weeks while searching for work.

Sitting in my chair reading messages from my emails in the hopes of coming across a job offer, I cannot help but feel a little drowsy. With the recent phone calls, my adventure at the Unemployment Office and anxious children running about, the toll becomes too great and I drift off into a nap I truly deserve.

4

I begin to dream and can hear soft tropical music, the same music that has haunted my mind since the last dream. I open my eyes to find myself in a familiar setting but again I am lost. Is this the island of despair, the island where I have lost my wife to the shadows of corporate big wigs, speaking of my fate?

Yes, this is the place. I can see the pier and the profile of fashionably attired men and woman enjoying themselves with cocktails and fine cuisine. The day is bright and sunny, and yes, there is Amy, my wife. She is walking towards me, the sea breeze blowing her hair in a soft wave like motion. She is wearing a summer dress, one that is very charming and yet polite to the eyes. She takes my hand and we begin to walk on the sand, towards the pier.

I squeeze her hand tightly, this time I am not going to lose her to the sounds and sights that fall before my eyes and ears. As we enter the pier, I am in awe by the business yet casual look of the surroundings. Across the way, I see the men who changed my life, once again waving for me to approach. As I make my way across the pier and through the maze of partygoers, I realize that Amy is nowhere in my presence. Again, I have lost her and yet, I must face the fear of the unknown. "What will I say, what do they want?"

Walking towards the group of individuals who have waved me over, I can see that once again they are ignoring me. I listen intently to their conversations and hear comments such as, "When will he learn, he does not need us?" I abruptly break into their chatter, at first polite and then in a more stern voice I cry out, "Why do you keep calling to me and inviting me to your group? Can you hear me?"

Just after shouting these words to the men among me, I notice the sea is becoming more violent. The wind picks up its strength and the waves begin to make their intrusion upon the pier. Blackness begins to fall across the sky and I race over to the railing and look out into the sea, concerned for the well-being of Amy and the strength of the storm. I turn from the railing of the pier and as I turn, my eyes begin to deceive me. I am alone, standing on the wooden platform that gave host to many a person just a few moments past.

The tables, the partygoers and the board of directors all gone, vanished from this place; however, I am not alone. There is a man standing at the far end of the pier, resting his hands on the railing and gazing out into the sea. I recognize him yet; I cannot seem to place his name. "Does he have a name?"

Dodging the wind and rain, I make my way to his side, calling out to him. Confused and frightened, I reach out to touch his shoulder and I close my eyes, not sure what to expect from his reaction to my grabbing hand. As I reach for his shoulder, I feel a fine material, the texture that only a man of his wealth and fortune can wear. The tension brought on by the storm and the fear that I have for this man's well being is too much to handle. I open my eyes and in my grasp is my five year olds baseball shirt. "Daddy, can you help me put on my baseball clothes?" he asks while shoving the uniform onto my lap.

Again, it was the dream. Trying hard to remember every vivid account of its detail seems impossible yet, I was remembering. I did remember the conversations from the group but "whom were they speaking about and what did they mean? Where did they go? Who was the man left behind on that stormy pier?" Maybe I was an outsider looking in; maybe I am seeing a glimpse into the future. Someone else in the office is going to follow my fate. Maybe that person grasping onto the railing, was he next?

"What ever," I mutter to myself, and then quickly remembering my five-year-old son and his determination for me to help him with his baseball uniform.

That evening my family and I are sitting on the bleachers watching my son's T-ball game, trying to avoid conversations with fellow spectators as well as each other. I feel a tap on my shoulder, startled I turn in my seat and notice Shaun, staring back at me. "Hello brother," he says looking at me as if now would be a good time for a Nancy explanation.

Shaun and I have been friends since elementary school and it only makes sense for us to address each other as brothers. I respond maintaining a tone in my voice as if everything is normal in my life, "Hi Shaun, long time no see."

"I've been calling your house for days and your never home. Doesn't Amy give you my messages?" Shaun asks in a low and concerning voice. "After all, we are the best of friends and nothing ever happens in our lives that one or the other is not aware." Realizing I cannot hide from the truth and must face my friends with the bitter news about my unemployment. I get up from my seat and walk Shaun to a more secluded section of the ball field. "The reason I have not been very social is that I had lost my job a few weeks ago…"

Shaun interrupts, "That's why you were at Nancy's alone and avoiding my phone calls." His voice seems more concerning than I would have expected. "Don't worry; you know Carla and I will help you and the kids. I don't want you to think its charity; after all we're more like family than just good friends." "I know but things may be looking up. I have an interview on Friday, so hopefully this storm will blow over."

Shaun puts his hand on my shoulder as a sign of reassurance. "The family is waiting for me in the car. Tommy had his game earlier and I am sure they will want to get something to eat on the way home. Good luck, and call me later. By the way, there is no need to go to Nancy's alone. I can always think of an excuse to down a few cocktails."

With those words, Shaun pats me on the shoulder and walks towards the parking lot, to his awaiting family. I return to my seat on the bleachers next to Amy watching the exciting world of Little League baseball. As I sit down Amy leans over and says, "What could be more important than watching your son's baseball game, Steve?" I look over and we both leer at each other with disgusted eyes. I am beginning to think this woman, my wife, is doing everything in her power to push me over the edge, circling around me waiting to strike and deliver the final blow.

I am briefly concerned that I may have told Shaun too much, too soon but now, after the conflict with Amy, I did not care who knew about our situation. Even though I had a true friendship with Shaun, I needed to find the bond that Amy and I once shared. I have despised her comments and questioning these past few weeks but I know she is the person that will help me through the tough times.

While pondering over these thoughts in my head, I hear her voice. "Do you think you could go to the concession stand and buy some popcorn and a soft drink for us without talking to everyone that you meet along the way?" I get up from the bleachers and make my way to the concession stand stopping to speak with whom ever will give me the time. As I make casual conversations along the way, I continually look back towards Amy hoping to catch her eye. Amy notices me visiting with other spectators and quietly mouths the words, "Grow up." Over the past few weeks, Amy and I have developed an art form for irritating one another, each of us trying to have the last word.

5

Friday morning, I awake from my sleep with the intentions of making the best impression possible; to a company I know nothing about, "Anyway, how can things go wrong? I am an experienced professional with a great work ethic, and I know that I will be a valuable asset to any organization." I happily think to myself, while basking in the warmth of my early morning shower.

The commute to the interview is uneventful and as I drive up to the building labeled with the address, I notice the name of the company, Global Technologies. Alas, I remember the position and why I had sent them a resume, this was going to be my new home. I feel back on track, no longer that jockey looking over his shoulder.

As I make my way into the office, I straighten my tie and align my hair, hoping to find the executive look that has me so longing to return. I make my way to the receptionist's desk and advise her that I am here for an interview.

"Here fill this form out and return it to me when you are finished," she directs in a stern voice, never once glancing up to make eye contact or, even acknowledging my existence. "Okay?" I respond with a puzzling voice. I move to a chair in the lobby and glance at the form, it is a one-page application. "Easy enough," I say to myself in a quiet voice.

As I begin to fill out the form, I realize that there is not enough space provided to accurately complete the information, and include the great reasons why I am the person for the position. Finally, I squeeze as much information onto the form and return it to the desk hoping that

I have written down the most pertinent information about my experience in relation to the position before me.

"Can I write on the back page or, add my resume to the application? There wasn't enough room to write." I ask, using my most professional demeanor. "No, we have already received your resume. How do you think we called you?" With that, she took the form and walked to the back room, disappearing into the complex maze of offices and cubicles.

I return to a seat in the lobby and wait for the announcement of my name. I am nervous and excited crossing my legs, uncrossing my legs, folding my hands and playing with the pleat on my pants leg, repeating these actions as a means of taking my mind away from the tension that surrounds me. Twenty minutes pass when I hear my name called, "Mr. Woods, will you follow me?" No offer of a handshake, no greeting, just a firm order from a man wearing a suit and tie yet, his look disorganized.

I follow him into a conference room adorned with many windows, the type of designs, which allow light to shine through and provide warmth, comfort and a scenic view of the landscaping. This room, however, felt cold and dreary and the only scenery to cross my gaze was that of a man reading and studying my resume as if he were looking at it for the first time. I quickly realize this will not be the day I have prayed for, these past few weeks.

Several minutes pass and we begin our conversation, a conversation that analyzes my skills and abilities. A one-sided meeting, explaining why he will not hire me as apposed to why I should get the job. The interview lasts about forty-five minutes and in that time, I have not only lost the job but also, started to feel as if this person were correct. "Did I have any skills or abilities? Was I the person for their company, any company?"

I left feeling overwhelmed, depressed and a man without answers. My stomach begins turning, I know that the reality of still being unemployed and facing my family when I return home this afternoon is a feeling I would not wish for my worst enemy. This was a new experience; I was the man of the house, the breadwinner and usually the decision maker. In my positions past, I had always been on top; always had an input in big decisions and most of my colleagues and subordinates looked up to me. "Who does this half-assed dressed man think he is?"

I regain my senses and quickly realize that he is the decision maker and for what it is worth, I can only hope to move on and find that golden career. I have to get back on track and find that one company that will show me the same gratitude and respect that I will reciprocate through my experience and hard work.

I take my suit coat off and hang it neatly on a hook in the back seat of the car. I get in and feel for my keys in my pants pocket, and nothing. "Do not tell me I left them in the office," I think to myself. Just like Nancy's, I will have to go into a place I do not feel welcomed and look for my keys. As I begin to exit the car, I can see the reflection from the sun light dancing off the metal key ring, lying on the floorboard. "Thank God," I mutter and I reach down to pick them up, thinking about what I could have ever done to these keys for them to treat me this way.

While reaching down to get the keys I can feel something lying on the floor just under the seat. I reach down to grab the keys and instead pull up a mysterious envelop containing a card inside. The envelope is addressed to me, in Amy's handwriting. "It is not Father's Day or, my Birthday. Is it our anniversary?" I think to myself wondering what surprise Amy has left for me to open. I open the card and it reads:

What ever happens big or small,
I will catch you when you fall!

Love,

Amy

Can I be so lucky? Can this woman be the person I married? For nine years she has stayed with me through the good times and the bad yet, she does not show her fears or uncertainties about our current situation. Yes, she has become bitter and bossy but she has never left my side. Maybe it is our sons, they keep her so busy that she relies on me to worry and plan for the both of us. I reach down again and pick up my keys, start the car and begin the long journey home, still unsure of what to tell Amy about the interview.

During the drive, my transient thoughts lead me into the parking lot of Nancy's. "Why would I come to this place?" I think as I maneuver through the parking lot unsure if I should park. I usually never drink alone but for some reason my mind feels that I should be here in this lot. We have been coming to Nancy's since college, all of us, me, my wife, and our good friends. It is as if the neighborhood and its inhabitants have used this bar and grill as not just an escape from life but also a place of new beginnings, a place where we started our new lives, to reflect on the past and plan for our futures.

Remember Shaun, he brings his new clients here, not so much because of the atmosphere but, because of what it represents and the good fortune we have been given throughout our lives. I turn the car around and exit the parking lot making my journey home. I am sure Amy is anxious about the interview after all, how could I deny her of my time when she has left me such a beautiful card?

I pull into the driveway and slip into the house, hoping that my presence will silently fade into the backdrop of the home activities. As I make my way into the den, BAM! Amy interrogates me with a thousand questions, "Did you get the job? Do you know that bill collectors are starting to call? Why are you not working yet? I am pregnant!"

"So much for the lovely card," I think as she asks the same questions repeatedly. Her interrogation is too much and I can only shout a response, "All right! All right, Amy!" Raising my voice and tossing my briefcase onto the floor of the kitchen I say, "Will you listen? No, I will probably not get the job! They told me that my salary expectations are too high and this position will be a step down from my previous employment."

I know Amy does not understand my explanations or the economic reasoning for decisions made by corporations, however, she never gives me the chance to share with her, information that I too am learning while searching for work. I guess I had forgotten about Mr. Bill Collector and at the time he called I was not too worried or upset after all, I did have this interview lined up.

"Anyone call while I was out?" I ask, trying to change the subject and regain some sense of authority. "No, no one called to offer you that great job that you so greatly deserve or, think you deserve. It has been two months now and you have only had one interview." Amy is relentless; I cannot get a word in edge wise as she stammers out of the room and up the stairs muttering words to herself that I can only hope not to hear.

"Daddy, are we poor?" asks our eight-year-old son who has just come from the living room watching his favorite cartoons. It seems that my wife and I have once again forgotten about the other ears in the house, during our arguing and screaming. I look at my son and give him the reassurance that everything will be all right, and that in no way will our lives change. "Now go and play with your brother and give Dad another hug." While hugging him I wonder if those words are the truth. "Will we be Okay?" I think to myself knowing that only time will tell.

6

As I mentally return to the interview with Olivia, I take a moment to ponder over the story that has come so easily to my lips. I glance up and notice Olivia writing as quickly as her hand will allow. "Do you need to take a break or use the restroom?" I ask, hoping that she will let me continue while the thoughts and feelings are still fresh in my mind. It appears that this interview is going well and if I am going to continue, I need her full attention.

"No thank you. Mr. Woods. Please, tell me about the products your company manufactures, the floats." Before she can finish her comments, I interrupt and reply, "Let me finish my story, I think that will answer your questions." She looks up at me as a sign to continue, taking her pen in hand and tentatively listens as I mentally slip away into the past.

"As I am lying in bed one evening staring at the ceiling for what seems like an eternity…"

Thoughts of despair and desperation race through my mind. Looking for work has proven to be a full time job; however, I am bored to tears. There are not enough projects to do around the house and I am starting to get in the way, more so than helping. It is true that absence does make the heart grow fonder and I know Amy could use a few days of solitude away from me.

"I'll write a book, a children's book! Where did that come from?" I think to myself, "What do I know about what children like? After all, I do have two sons and one child on the way." I lie in bed thinking of a

theme for my book, "Let's see, think, think, think." I repeat to myself, while staring at the rotation of the ceiling fan blades above. I quietly get out of bed and head to the den where I do all of my best thinking.

As I sit in my chair I cannot help but laugh, thinking about the geese in our neighborhood and how bold and brave they seem to be…Walking and sleeping in the middle of the street, chasing people away when all they want to do is provide an offering of breadcrumbs from the cupboard. "That is it, a children's story about Gambling Geese," and I begin to type.

The Gambles are a family of geese that have made their home near a pond in an area of town known as Cliché. Ironically enough, its name comes from the French word-meaning stereotype. The Gambles have called this little patch of land home for nearly four flocks, or four generations. They go about their day, as Geese tend to do eating, swimming and sunning themselves on dry, warm cement. Other flocks in the neighborhood are more cautious than the Gamble's. They stay near the pond and take food and crumbs from any small child or any interested person that will come their way.

As winter begins to draw near the other flocks laugh and sing nasty songs about the Gambles, and the silly things they do for survival. The other flocks at the pond often-hold wagers as to which Gamble will be hit by the passing cars on the roadway. Gary Gamble always tells his children not to accept food from the humans, and as for resting on the warm cozy streets, well it only makes sense. He always says, "We have the skills and patients to find food and the sense to stay on the side of the road. Yes we may take chances that the other flocks will never consider but, we are more dependant and ready to face tough times that may come our way."

One day while members of other flocks listen to Gary give his famous speech to his children, parents from other flocks gather around and begin to mock his ideas, and they chant, "Gary Goose has a few screws loose! Gary Goose has a few screws loose!" Repeatedly they sing as they waddle off to the pond in melodious harmony. "We'll show you Gambles!" One goose yells, as they waddle off into the distance.

"Do not bother listening to the other flocks children, for winter grows upon us and we must make our nest ready with food and shelter." Gary affirms with an authoritative voice.

Winter approaches and the people stop coming to the pond with food and crumbs for the geese and the nests alone cannot provide the warmth the geese so desire. The other flocks were nervous, they had waited too long to fly South for the winter and they need to eat and warm their beds.

The leaders of the other flocks gather for a meeting, a meeting to vent their frustrations and to seek advices from the eldest of the flocks. "It seems to me that we regain our strength by using the warm pavement to rest our cold bones and find a new source of food," cries one of the elders while preaching to the crowd as he paces along the banks of the pond. The others agree but who will test the pavement? Only the Gambles have survived the racing of cars on the streets and they have always chased away the feeders at the pond. Can it be that their gambling ways have made them a stronger flock?

The idea seems ridiculous yet, with nothing else on their side except a gamble, one selected member from among the flocks sets his naive feet upon the pavement and begins to cross the road. "Ah, this does feel nice on the feathers!" He cries out to the other flocks, and with that remark, he is flattened by an on coming car. The other flocks gasp at the site while the Gambles just shake their heads in mournful respect.

One of the elders cries out to Gary and asks for help. Gary quickly waddles over to the side of the road and replies, "You have never taken a risk, you have relied on feeders to bring crumbs and bread to the pond, and when the seasons change from summer to winter you do not take time to find warmth amongst the cars on the road. Because of this, you are not prepared to survive in this pond throughout the entire year. Us Gambles have always honked and chased our feeders, forcing us to find our own food. As well, we have learned that staying on the side of the road will almost *always avoid a dreadful accident and yet, provide us with the warmth we need to be strong."*

After Winter had come and gone, the remaining flocks that had survived the harshness of the season use Gary's advise and teach their families and new flocks at the pond the valuable lessons of independence and taking chances that may one day save their lives.

The End

I sit back into my chair looking at my masterpiece. "Is this a child's book?" It seems so harsh and adult like in nature. I continue thinking, "Did I write a story about me, for me? Do I take chances? Have I not always depended on the safety of my career and my surroundings?"

As I dwell on these questions, I begin to wonder if I am loosing my mind, I need a job and I need one fast. As much as I love my family, I need to be out of the house and soon, at least before my wife kicks me out. I look at the clock, one-thirty in the morning; I wonder where the time has gone. Sitting back in my chair, I can feel my eyelids growing heavy, I hope to dream of my children and the happy times we have had and will have in the years to come, and just like that, I fade to sleep.

The Thrill of Victory

7

The crashing of waves and the rumble of thunder are over powering the soft tropical music that once filled the atmosphere of my dreams. I look around, it is dark, and the moonlight peeking through the clouds gives me enough light to see the events taking place in my very presence. I am standing at the entrance of the pier, the same pier that haunts my dreams. I adjust my sight and mind to the surroundings and see a man standing on the edge of the pier. He is the man that I had left alone, standing and looking out into the horizon as if he had lost something or someone and was awaiting for its return. The waves are crashing up and over the rails as if to be pulling him into the water. I cry out to him, "Sir, sir I will help you! Hang on, don't let go!"

As I run towards the end of the pier, it seems to be getting longer and I cannot seem to make my way to him. Fighting the wind and rain, I finally reach the man putting out my hand once again to grab hold of his clothing. He is wearing a black suit and yet, with the wind and rain I can see that his hair is not out of place.

With the blink of an eye, the waves reach up and grab him as if to say, "Too late, he is mine," and into the abyss, he falls. As I climb up and lean over the railing to assist the poor soul, I notice he is falling backwards and looking at me with an intense emptiness in his eyes showing no signs of resistance or any effort to save himself.

I study the man's face as he drifts farther and farther from my sights. Suddenly I recognize the identity of this fallen stranger and I scream in horror, "Oh my God, it's me!" It cannot be, what possible event could this man have experienced that he would plummet into the sea and seal his own doom. I extend my hand as a gesture of help but there is no reaction from the fallen stranger. He continues to fall deeper and deeper into the blackness, and then he is lost.

There is a loud clash of thunder and I arise from my chair startled, not by the noise outside my window but by the vision of my dream. I am soaking in sweat and tears, worried about what this dream could be telling me. What will happen if I close my eyes again? I make my way from the den to the couch and with an exhausted thump; I drift off until morning, giving in to the melodious rhythm of the rain on the living room windows.

Weeks go by, it is now mid-summer still, no job leads and the relationship between my wife and I are straining. I begin to loose faith in myself becoming bitter and worn and it cannot be easy for Amy, coping with pregnancy, raising two children and learning to live with a man she thought she once knew.

The telephone rings and there is but a brief slimmer of hope that this call will be for me, possibly a response from one of the hundreds of resumes that I have sent to unsuspecting companies, however, the call is for Amy. I can hear that she is conversing with Shaun's wife, Carla and I strain to listen to their conversation. I try not to be a nosey husband but her conversation with Carla seems to eliminate my boredom, which has overtaken me these last few months.

The phone call ends and I hear Amy ask the children if they would like to go for a swim in Shaun and Carla's pool. I put my head down knowing that Amy will ask me to attend. "I don't feel like a social gathering, pretending to be someone I'm not, or acting as if nothing happened and my life is perfect!" I shout from the other room waiting for a sympathetic response. Amy responds while gathering the children's pool attire, "I never invited you!"

I get up from the couch and walk into the kitchen and for the first time since the pregnancy I notice my wife and how beautiful she is, glowing and showing. I think to myself, "How long has it been since the news? Can she be this far along in her pregnancy?"

"Here, let me carry the beach bags over to Shaun's house," I say in an apologetic voice. "Fine," she adds but in such an impersonal way that I begin to realize that the past few months have taken a toll on her person, our marriage.

The bright sun and clean air begins to clear my head, maybe it is the abusive use of chlorine Shaun uses in his pool, nonetheless, I begin to feel as if there are going to be changes in our lives, thinking to myself sipping on a margarita that Carla has made for the group. Reclining back in the lounge chair, I become mesmerized, watching my wife and children in the pool playing, swimming and occasionally arguing over the many pool toys that float about.

I notice Amy trying to get onto a float in the pool but with no luck. "What's the matter babe? Is your belly keeping you down?" I shout but not without a giggle from Shaun and Carla. Amy frustratingly replies, "No, I'm trying to lie on my side so I can get some sun on my back. I can't lie on my belly and I don't want to look half tan and half white!" "Why don't you cut out the center and...?"

At this moment realizing what I am about to say, I stop just in time as to keep it a secret, I begin to envision a pool float for expectant mothers. That was it but, how do I get started, who should I call?

That evening, rushing into the house and sitting behind my desk I begin to finalize the float, drawing rough sketches on paper researching information on patents and printing multiple copies of contact information from my computer. "Can it be, a man from the mid-west having an idea that can be U.S. patented?" There was not any planning involved, I did not spend days developing a product, it just came to me, as quickly and quietly as a dream.

Later that evening I found myself pacing the floor of my den, thinking and planning. No, not about the invention, rather, how will I convince Amy to let me spend the money we so desperately need to sustain our lives, on a risk where there are no guarantees for success? Walking from wall to wall and making the turn more times than I can remember, I hear Amy coming down the stairs. She has just put our sons to bed and would begin her evening ritual; looking through magazines, flipping through the channels in search of those ridiculous reality shows that have seemed to monopolize evening programming and painting her nails. I walk out of my den and meet her halfway down the hall. "Hello dear," I say while giving her a much overdue kiss on the lips. "I want to discuss something with you that will help us get back on track," I add hoping to seal the deal with that one sentence.

"Okay, let's talk in the kitchen I need to finish the dishes," Amy replies as if she had heard my words yet, had other things on her mind. I follow her into the kitchen, much as if a child would follow his or her parent after a harsh scolding.

Amy goes about the kitchen taking plates and bowls from the dishwasher and placing them back into their respective cabinets while I gather up the strength to pursue her approval.

"I have and idea rather, an invention I would like to have patented." I say, waiting and listening for the laughing of disapproval, however, there is no laugh and she actually looks at me as if she is telling me to continue. I take her hand and lead her to the table saying, "Sit down and listen to my idea."

She takes a seat and stares at me with piercing eyes as I continue to explain my pool float idea and as I begin to speak, I start pacing around the kitchen much like a defense attorney in court, trying to convince a jury or judge that his case is solid.

After explaining the idea and the financial investment of chasing this venture, Amy gets up from the table; walks over to me and kisses my cheek as a sign of her consent. "If you think this idea will work and you can find a way to make it happen, I will support your decision."

"I have won but it did not seem like much of a fight," I thought to myself feeling that this was too easy a victory. Did she give her approval to avoid an argument? After all, my wife will stare at a cash register at the grocery or any retail outlet for that matter, while the prices of goods are being tallied, watching every product as it runs through the scanner. If she caught a mistake, well let us just say that I have seen the strongest and bravest of cashier's fall trembling to their knees over an error of a few cents.

I can only think that like me, Amy is frustrated with our situation and feels that there are no other options but for us to take the risk. Either way, I was ready to move forward.

"Thank you honey, for your support and you won't be sorry, I think it is a great idea. And any way, with all the crap that's sold today, why not add to the fodder." I replied and walked down the hall to my den but not without bursting aloud, "Just call me Gary Goose!" "What?" I hear Amy respond from the kitchen. I shout back to her, "Nothing honey, nothing at all."

The next day I pick up the telephone and dial a number that will change our lives forever. "Hello, Richard Charm attorney at law…" I explain my situation to Mr. Charm and the idea that I would like to have patented. He advises me that I will receive paperwork from his office that I must complete and mail back to him, immediately. I listen intently to everything he says regarding patents and make notes for my records. After our conversation, I hang up the phone and lean back in my chair. I fold my hands on the back of my head and smile for I have made the first step towards making my dreams come true.

8

These next few months have quickly come and gone and my wife is expecting to deliver our third child, in a few weeks. "Oh, and I have found a job," yes, I said a job. The hard work and many hours spent looking for that golden career, has been for naught.

It seems that many companies in this great land of opportunity are not seeking individuals with creativity or a good work ethic but those that will bid the lowest salary. Therefore, the career will have to wait for now, as I need to help my wife with her duties at home and her preparations for the arrival of our new baby.

As I sit and rot at a job that has no future, I begin to fantasize about my U.S. Patent, imagining the satisfaction of producing a product that I have developed and selling that product in retail outlets to consumers. I am lost in deep thought when the ringing of the telephone upon my desk awakes me into reality. Two lines are ringing simultaneously and I pick up the first line sending the other into my voicemail.

"Hello, this is Steve." "Steve, Mr. Charm, your patent attorney," the voice on the other line reports.

"Oh yes, hello. What is the good news? Have you heard about my patent?" I anxiously reply. Mr. Charm answers, "Yes, it has been approved and your invention is now patent pending. Congratulations and I wish you luck!" "Patent pending?" I respond as if asking a question. "Yes, Mr. Woods, it can take a couple of years or longer to have a patent issued on your product but, no worries. There isn't another product similar to yours filed with the U.S. Patent Office, so feel free to begin the manufacturing details, if you wish." I anxiously reply, "Thank you, good news at last!"

During our short conversation, I had forgotten that the second line was ringing and the light on my voicemail is flashing. Anyway, who cares I have a patent pending product, "Floating for Two", the pool float for expectant mothers.

I was so proud of this idea after all; the float was your average pool float with one underlying benefit. The removable center will allow an expectant mother to lie in the prone position while tanning on her back. When the expectant mother is not using the float, the center can be snapped back into place offering recreational enjoyment of fun in the sun by anyone; men, women and children. No more one-sided tans for these mothers-to-be, they will now have the option to lie on their backs or on their bellies.

The marketing concept will be simple water parks, theme parks, maternity stores as well as any retail outlet that can benefit from a multi-purpose pool float. Oh, life is looking good and I finally feel as if my creativity and experiences are paying off and I will soon reap the rewards for my hard work and sacrifice. I realize that I have a lot of work ahead of me and seeking the interest of manufacturers will not be an easy task. I am facing two questions, do I produce the pool floats myself; on the other hand, do I hope to find a manufacturer that will be interested in paying royalties to me, for the idea? I have plenty of research ahead of me but for now, I must concentrate on the tasks at hand, my job and listening to the voicemail left during my conversation with Mr. Charm.

While dialing the access code to my voicemail the line on my telephone rings once again. Still basking in the glow of success, I calmly answer, "Good afternoon and how can I help you today?" "Steven, it's me, Amy. I've got something to tell you." "I do too my sweet and I…Hey wait a minute are you crying?" I listen intently for the sound of sniffles and then a sob.

"What's wrong? Is everything Okay?" I inquire anxiously afraid to hear her response. "I went to the doctor's office today for my last check-up and Dr. Weber thinks there is something wrong with the baby's heart." Amy spoke as if she had to pull herself together to tell me this horrific news.

I sink into my office chair as all the happiness and joy leave my body nothing at this moment seems to matter anymore, the job, the patent. Only what was happening to my unborn child and what I will sacrifice to make everything okay. I begin to reason with myself, "Could I be so lucky? It does not seem fair or even practical; my other two children are healthy as horses." I am in such a deep trance that I forget my wife is on the other line waiting for a reply.

"Steve, Steve!" Amy shouts in despair trying to get my attention. "I have a doctor's appointment in one hour and I need you to be there with me." I immediately respond, "Yes, I will be there." "Oh, what was it that you had to tell me, Steve?" she quizzically asks.

I answer, not wanting to change the subject but hoping that this bit of news will somehow cheer her up. "Well, I received a call from my patent attorney a few moments ago and Floating for Two has been approved for patent pending status." I cannot pretend to be happy over my news and I add, "But that's not important right now, I will see you in one hour, Oh, and I love you."

I hang up the telephone and sit behind my desk feeling afraid, helpless, and even lonely. Holding back the tears that long to flow, I walk into my manager's office and advise him that I will be leaving for the day, a personal matter.

It is hard for me to feel like Gary the gambling goose after all, his life seems so perfect and planned, ready for any occasion, in good times and in bad. Well, that is not me, I am not, and could never prepare myself for the news that my wife has dropped on me. Nothing can ever prepare a person for this type of news.

The closer to the doctor's office I get, the more afraid I become and as I park my car, I have to gather every bit of strength to walk into the building. I am nervous about what I might find, a hysterical wife crying and sobbing of the news we may receive from the exam. I scan the waiting room and notice Amy sitting in a chair reading a magazine and to my surprise; she is as calm as the island breeze that has plagued my dreams so many times these past few months.

"Hello dear," I say to her as I bend down to give her a small kiss on the cheek. "I'm glad you made it, they should be calling us into the room any minute." Sure enough as Amy says those words, the door opens and a nurse walks into the waiting room calling her name. "Amy Woods, Amy Woods." The nurse smiling as she looks around the room to make eye contact with someone responding to her call. This was the first time that I hated hearing the sound of my wife's name; it was a shock to my system.

We begin the long journey to the exam room and I realize that this may be a new beginning, a new chapter in our lives. I can only imagine what problems lie in wait for my unborn child. Heart surgeries, hospital stays, not being able to live a normal childhood and I cannot rule out the worst-case scenario, death.

I gather up the little strength I have left and follow my wife into the exam room, mentally preparing myself for some of the worst news a dad can receive. The next few moments seem to be a blur as I watch the specialist examine the baby's heart using ultra-sound imaging and only responding to his findings with an occasional, "I see." These responses have kept me in the dark for the past fifteen minutes and I cannot take the fear of the unknown any longer. I blurt out in frustrated anger, "Tell me doctor what's wrong? Is the baby going to be okay?"

I look at my wife as tears begin to collect in the corners of her eyes as the doctor replies, "Absolutely." Realizing that he may have kept us at bay longer than necessary he says, "The reason for the scare was that during the initial ultra-sound earlier today, your doctor interpreted a reading that he thought could possibly be a malfunction in the heart but, as it turns out it was just a shadow and everything is fine."

I cannot believe my ears, am I this upset that the visit to the doctor's office was only a scare? Am I elated with joy that everything is as it should be? Again, more questions for my mind and no answers to bring any relief. If there was ever a moment in our lives that allowed Amy and I to let go of our emotions and feelings, to relieve the stress that has built up within us over the past few month, this would be the moment. The defining point in our marriage where we both realize what really matters in our lives. I lay my head on my wife's belly and we begin to sob like infants, our hands engaged in a grasp that could only be broken by the strength of our love. Quietly, the doctor and nurses clean the room and leave us to our privacy.

After what seems like an eternity, I lift my head and look at my wife. Even though we have both been sobbing, she has managed to pull herself together, regaining her composure. Almost as if she knows that, there is still work to be done at home and other children to tend. Myself, I look as if a train has run me over and backed up to finish the job. I realize Amy is more powerful than I can ever become, not just at this moment but also, in every aspect of her life physically, emotionally and mentally.

For the past few months she has taken care of our sons, dealt with the ups and downs of pregnancy, took the phone calls from bill collectors and most importantly, she tolerated my childish and selfish behaviors. Yes, I admit that I had not been the easiest person to live with during these last few months of uncertainties. The credit for our stability will have to go to Amy, my wife and hero.

Amy drives home from the doctor's office, I cannot gather the strength or concentration to sit behind the wheel of a car and I would rather spend the time with my wife sharing the day's events and celebrating the news we have just received. We leave my car at the doctor's office, in the parking lot and head home. During the ride, we engage in small talk never really discussing the doctor's visit, it was as if we both wanted to pretend the fear of the unknown during our short visit to the doctor's office was nothing more than a test. Testing the strength of our marriage, one that I am not sure I could have passed with any other person.

I lay my head back against the seat and contemplate on the day's events and the overwhelming feeling of relief that has set in. Knowing that our unborn child will be healthy, I begin to focus my discussion with Amy on the pool floats and the avenues we can take finding a manufacturer.

9

Two weeks pass and there are no responses from potential manufacturers regarding the letters I have sent about the floats. I am growing impatient and wondering if the same companies that were discarding my resumes were having an input into my queries to pool float producers.

While surfing the internet the telephone rings and by now, I have become so complacent that I no longer wonder if it is the call that I have been longing to hear these past few months. I pick up the receiver and without any thought I answer, "Hello." As I listen for a response the unfamiliar voice replies, "May I speak to Steve?" "Speaking," I respond afraid of who is on the other end of the call. "This is Rick Jamison with Water Products and we have received your letter regarding a pool float for expectant mothers."

I am stunned, a manufacturer interested in my patent. "Yes, how are you?" I say excitedly yet, maintaining a sense of professionalism. "I'm fine; I would like to hear more about the product at a trade show in New York City next week. Do you think you can attend?"

I am amazed unable to register everything the man is telling me. I calmly regain my composure and begin to chat with the gentleman for a brief period. We discuss royalty programs, production and marketing for the pool floats all within a matter of a few moments. I write down the information for the Outdoor Products Trade Show and advise him that I will attend.

We finish our conversation and I hang up the telephone jumping into the air, clapping my hands and falling on my knees to give the family dog a hug she will never forget. I am the only one home and can hardly wait to tell Amy that our ship has finally come in.

I pace the house bursting to tell someone of my good fortune, walking back and forth until I remember Shaun. I will tell Shaun the good news after all, he will be more than happy for us and interested in what I have to say. I pick up the phone and call his office, while the receptionist transfers my call to Shaun's desk I repeatedly say to myself, "Please be there, please."

"This is Shaun," he answers in his professional tone. "It's Steve; I've got some interesting news." "Hello Steve, what's the good word?" He responds giving me his full attention. I begin to explain the phone call from Water Products and the trip I will be taking to New York City. As we are conversing, Amy walks through the front door, returning from her errands.

I tell Shaun that I will discuss the trade show in more detail later that evening, at Nancy's. Amy is home and I do not want her to think I am telling everyone else before I tell her the good news. I make my way down the hall towards Amy and say, "Honey, I have good news. Put down your bags and come to the kitchen!" "What is it?" she replies setting bags down onto the table.

"I received a call from Water Products a few moments ago and they want to hear more about Floating for Two." "Really," she replies skeptical that I am setting her up for a cruel joke. "I have to go to New York City next week to attend a trade show and present the product at their booth," I continue knowing what she will say next.

"How are we going to afford that trip?" she says anxious to hear my reply. "This feels like the sure thing. I know you will disagree but I am going to use the credit cards. I can find a cheap airfare rate and I will stay at a low class hotel. You have to trust me; the guy from Water Products sounds pretty convincing about wanting to produce the floats."

Later that evening I meet Shaun at Nancy's for some drinks and a further explanation of the trade show in New York. As we enter the doors, I begin to push through the crowd of patrons and head towards our favorite table in the back of the bar. As we approach, we notice that the bar seems extremely crowded and of course, other patrons are occupying our table. Realizing that we will have to find a new spot to sit this evening, I nod over to the bar and once again, we push through the crowd making our way to the counter.

As I order two drinks, Shaun says, "Who's going with you?" "Going where?" I ask but then remembering my New York trip. "I'm sorry; I guess I'm going alone. I can handle it; I have traveled all over the world, I think I can handle New York." Shaun takes a sip of his drink and replies, "No, no you cannot go alone. You need someone to watch your back, someone to be your tour guide." I look at him unsure of what he is saying as he continues, "I have already talked to Amy and before you had a chance to book your flight, I made reservations for us with my frequent flyer miles." Shaun holds his glass up to me and we toast the voyage that we will soon be undertaking.

I am happy again, or, at least content for the time. The thoughts of having a large bank account or seeing my product in market do not seem to excite me, there is still something missing, an emptiness that I cannot explain. I do not dwell on these thoughts for long, soon Shaun is buying another round and the void that I am feeling is replenished with the fine spirits that are working feverishly to satisfy my mind and taste buds.

As I continue telling my story to Olivia, there is a knock on the door and in a matter of seconds, Shaun peers his head into my office. "Shaun, come in. I would like you to meet someone," I say standing from my desk and stretching my legs. "Hi Steve, sorry for the interruption, I need to give you these reports before our sales meeting Monday. These are the projected numbers for next quarter."

After saying those words, Shaun looks at Olivia and back at me as if asking for an introduction. I take into consideration the hint and say, "I'm sorry, Olivia this is Shaun, my partner and Shaun this is Olivia."

"Nice to meet you, I have heard a lot about you today," she replies. Shaun looks at me with puzzling eyes as I continue to speak, "Oh, I'm sorry. I was telling her the inspirational story about Floating for Two and I was just about to continue with our New York trip. Olivia is writing a paper for a business course at the University and she is asking for the inspiration for our products."

Shaun sits down in a chair next to Olivia as if he too is waiting for me to continue. "I love this story. Please Steve, continue." "Thanks Shaun, I don't mind if I do," I reply sitting back down in my chair and straitening my tie. "The days leading up to our trip to New York seem to drag on…"

I am no longer anticipating phone calls from potential employers, now my focus is strictly on the trade show and the royalties I will receive. I am embarking on a journey that will begin my financially successful life.

Sitting aboard the plane that will take me to the Promised Land, I begin to fidget in my seat and Shaun can see that my nerves are getting the better of me. "What's the matter, are you afraid to fly?" he asks with a smirk on his face. "No, I just prefer to drive, that's all," I reply gathering up the strength to look him in the eyes. I have been on airplanes many times but I still cannot bring myself to enjoy the experience. Shaun, still concerned with my uneasiness grabs my hand and looks me square in the face. He begins to speak in a serious tone, "If something happens to the plane, we will hold hands and look deeply into each other's eyes." As he finishes those words he bursts into laughter and continues, "Lighten up Steve, you big baby."

At the hotel in New York, Shaun and I notice the elegance and historical theme surrounding the lobby. We check in and make our way to the room, taking the elevator up to the twelfth floor. "I thought you booked a cheap hotel?" Shaun asks while admiring the couch placed against the back of the elevator and the fur rug placed in the center of the elevator floor. As I too stare at the couch and fur rug I answer, "I did, this was recommended by the Water Products Company and we got the trade show discount rate, I think."

As the elevator doors open, we step out and begin to make our journey down the hall, passing elegant oak trim doors and the myriad of statues that line the corridor. "Here it is room 1207," I say to Shaun while placing my key into the door hoping that our room is just as elegant.

I allow Shaun to enter first and I quickly follow taking in the many amenities for our disposal. As I am looking over my shoulder at the marble bathroom on my left, I suddenly run into the back of Shaun. "Why did you stop?" Before I could say anymore, I see Shaun standing still, pointing his finger into the main quarters of the room. "No wonder you got such a great deal, look."

As sure as I was standing there, I notice the thing that has stopped Shaun dead in his tracks. There is only one bed, sitting in the middle of the room adjacent to a large picture window that gives way to a glorious view of the city. "That's bullshit, I asked for two beds when I made the reservations. I'll call the front desk and let them know we need a cot."

We quickly reassure ourselves that we will not have to sleep together in the same bed and begin discussing our plans for the evening. Not soon after there comes a knock on the door. "That was quick," I think to myself. "That must be the cot," I say aloud making my way past the bathroom that Shaun has now occupied preparing for our night out.

I open the door and standing before me is a little old woman wearing a housekeeping uniform, clasping her hands together as if in prayer. "You like room?" she says in very broken English. I respond, "Yes, I like the room very much but, I called a few moments ago and requested a cot." She continues looking at me as if she understands my every word as I say, "There are two of us and only one bed. I need a cot." She nods her head as a sign that she understands, turns and walks down the hall.

I close the door, turn and walk back into our single bed bungalow to tell Shaun the good news. I do not get very far and he is walking towards me ready to see the sights opening his wallet to verify he's financially ready to have a good time. "Let's go, I've never been to New York and we have a lot to see and plenty to drink."

"Let me change my clothes then we can head out and by the way, the maid came to the door while you were in the bathroom and I told her to bring us a cot." "Good," Shaun replies, "I would hate to flip a coin to see which one of us is going to sleep on that lovely sofa in the elevator." We both laugh as I continue to unpack; I know it is going to be a long night and an early morning so I dress in the most comfortable attire I can find.

Not ten minutes have passed and again, a knock on the door. Shaun yells from the bathroom, "I'll get the door, hurry up and change!" A few seconds pass and while I am changing, I hear Shaun calling me to the door where he and the hotel's housekeeper are standing. She has an innocent smile on her face and Shaun appears to be confused. "What's the problem?" I say, making my way towards them. "Steve, she keeps nodding and smiling. I'm not sure what she wants." I look at the housekeeper then peer into the hall but there is no cot within my sight. "Any luck with the cot?" I ask, puzzled about her visit. She nods and holds up her hand showing me a box of tampons. She attempts to turn them over to me moving her hand towards mine. I tighten every muscle in my face not to laugh or embarrass the poor creature who has gone out of her way to bring me this package. "No, no. I need a cot. There are two men in this room. I would like to have a cot."

Once again I explain our situation yet the miscommunication becomes too much to bare. I politely push the box away and backup into my room, shutting the door. "What ever," I say looking at Shaun as we both begin to laugh hysterically. "What is it with woman and their applicators?" I say aloud and shaking my head in disbelief. Shaun looks puzzled and asks, "What do you mean?"

I explain how Amy told me she was pregnant and how she held up the pregnancy test two inches from my face. We both laugh some more and finish preparing for the long evening ahead.

Once we make our way to the lobby, we hail a cab and instruct the driver to take us to a nice steak house. We have not eaten since breakfast and are ready to dine on fine New York cuisine. As we are sitting in the cab Shaun looks over at me and says, "I'm glad to see that you have found your sense of humor. I was beginning to worry about your sanity."

"What's not to be happy about? A new baby soon and my financial problems seem to be fading away. Soon, I will be the pool float king." "You know Steve; I wouldn't count your chickens before they hatch. A lot can happen and there hasn't been any real discussion about the float or any contracts offered." I did not like that one thing about Shuan's personality, his brutal honesty. We loved each other like brothers; however, he was always showing me the alternative to any situation. "I know, I know. Let us hope these next few days are worth the trip, if not, I'd better find and apartment and become a seed in The Big Apple.

The cab driver pulls up along side the curb and in a soft tone says, "This is a good place to eat; I think you will like the atmosphere." From the backseat of the cab, we both look over to our left and peer into the large windows surrounding the restaurant. "Steve, do you notice anything unusual about this place?" Shaun asks, still peering from the back seat of the cab.

I take a few more moments to investigate the surroundings within the restaurant. "Nothing unusual except that it appears to be catering to all men." I say, noticing the cabby is becoming impatient with our exited delay. "Sir, we would prefer something with more of a night life. You know women, dancing, drinking and good food. This appears to be a...." Before I can finish my sentence, he adds, "Okay, hookers and cheeseburgers, coming up."

Shaun and I turn towards each other with a scared look in our eyes as we notice the taxi driver chuckling to himself." He pulls away from the curb and continues down the busy streets of New York passing our hotel and stopping at the next block. We look over to our right and see multiple neon signs, fancy eateries and plenty of people walking the streets having the time of their life. The driver stays facing forward as we pay the bill and exit the car.

"That asshole new all along where we wanted to go and he just made twelve dollars driving us in circles." The frustration in Shaun's voice was somewhat funny, after all, we are tourists and for what it's worth, ignorance comes with a price.

The rest of the night is filled with drinking, eating and visiting the many nightclubs the big city has to offer. Never once do we glance at our watches to check the time, nor do we care. We are two friends, letting loose and forgetting the day to day struggles that challenge our lives.

Early the next morning we awake feeling better than we had both predicted the night before. Some of last evening's events are still a bit foggy in my mind but today is a new day and I have to look good and make a great impression with my potential manufacturer.

We arrive at the trade show, enter our names on the list and make our way through the convention hall. Miles of booths and products litter the arena and everywhere we look, manufacturers are bidding with buyers and customers are negotiating pricing and terms with manufacturers. This is the outdoors product Mecca and I am an inventor. I walk the aisles looking at products even taking samples of goods many of the vendors are offering as gifts. Weaving in and out, dodging the thousands of people who are in attendance but throughout the chaos I cannot locate the company that is seeking my audience.

I feel a tap on my shoulder and turn around, Shaun has gotten my attention and for good reason. There, two aisles over, the most beautiful sign I have ever seen, right before my eyes. Water Products, the name I was longing to find within this large convention center. There seems to be a glow encircling their booth, a light reflecting beautifully from the ground to the ceiling. Yes, it was calling my name and for the first time since my lay off, I feel successful. Shaun and I make our way over to the space reserved for Water Products and yes, there is a glow. A glow caused by light reflecting from water in a pool, which has been installed specifically for the trade show.

I have to say that by now I am growing unusually nervous about my meeting after all; my life and my family's financial future are riding on this one particular meeting. Standing and gazing at the different products hung about and floating on the water, I hear a familiar voice. "Can I help you gentlemen?"

I turn and see a young man standing before us, dressed in kaki shorts and a golf shirt bearing his companies logo. "I'm Steve Woods. I have scheduled a meeting with Mr. Jamison regarding a pool float for expectant mothers that I have designed." The man shakes my hand and introduces himself as Mr. Jamison, the person who called me not more than a week ago. Whether he knows it or not, this man, his company is going to change my life. "Good to meet you. I have seen some schematics of your design so today I would like to speak with you on issues that concern our company. Follow me; I have set aside a small private tent for purchasers and others to speak in private, I think it may be vacant now."

Shaun and I follow him into a tent housing one small table and a few chairs set out for any awaiting business that may take place. "Steve, let me cut to the chase. Our concern is that your product is patent pending, therefore, no real protection until you receive final notice from the U.S. Patent Office. At first, I was under the impression that you held the patent rights which is why I telephoned you last week."

I begin to sink deeply into my chair, my stomach beginning to turn and I can almost feel Shaun staring at me as if to say, "I told you so." Mr. Jamison continues as my world once again begins to crumble beneath my weary legs, "We are still interested in the product, however; we are going to put your design on the back burner for awhile maybe a year or two." Finishing his remarks, I sit looking at him, listening but not hearing what he is saying. I strain the muscles in my face to maintain a smile as if to say I understand, however, no words come to my lips; I have lost the motivation to speak or even pretend to comprehend the words laid out before me.

"We understand. Please keep us in mind when your company makes a change. Also, we will let you know when the patent number is issued." Again, I hear voices but I am not making a sound, Shaun has stepped in and played the roll of my assistant, maintaining a forum of business during these past few moments. Realizing that I was not happy with the news that I had just received Mr. Jamison says, "I understand you made the trip to New York and believe me, we are still interested in the product. You have to understand, our CFO will not pay royalties to someone if there is no guarantee that a patent will be issued."

I cannot sit under this tent any longer and Shaun makes the first move to end the meeting realizing that he should remove me from the area before I say or do something that will end any future with Water Products. We stand, shake hands with Mr. Jamison and in a rather quick manner, we leave his presence.

Shaun and I continue walking aimlessly around the trade show trying to put the meeting behind us. Shaun experiments with new products while I try to remember what I have done in the past to deserve the lack of respect and lack of acknowledgment that I have been feeling these past few months. Repeatedly I think that this is the end, it is gutter city and I have to be the one to tell Amy.

The rest of the day and into the next, Shaun and I never mention the meeting to each other. Probably because he did not want to bring up a sore subject and I wanted to forget the embarrassment that I felt for bringing him half way across the country and bragging about my future riches. Still, explaining the trip to Amy will not be easy and I do not want to put any more pressure on her since she was so close to delivery, however, I know that I will have to drop the bomb before I arrive home.

With our trip ending, I decide to call Amy from the airport and explain to her that we will not be coming into money any time soon. I tell Shaun that I am going to use the restroom and to watch my bags. He nods his acknowledgement not taking his eyes away from a magazine he had picked up at the trade show.

I make my way through the terminal and step outside, dialing my home number from my cell phone. The telephone at my house rings for a few moments and I hear her lovely voice, however, it is the answering machine. "Amy, this is Steve. We are at the airport and it looks like we will be arriving on time. I can't wait to see you and the kids." I pause for a brief moment and I begin to speak, telling her of the meeting and Water Products hesitation for producing the float. I find myself stopping to hold back the tears of failure and despair as I finish and hang up the phone.

Collecting myself, I walk back into the terminal making my way towards the gate. In an odd way, I feel relief knowing that she will not have to hear the words directly form my lips. Hours will pass until I see Amy again, hopefully allowing the time she needs to deal with her anger towards our situation and the outcome of this trip.

On the plane, Shaun looks over at me and finally breaks the silence that has over shadowed us most of the day. He says in a sincere tone, "That was a great trip. Thanks for letting me tag along." I look over at him as he continues, "Just think we finally got to spoon together in bed. Who would have thought?" Those words, that voice, I begin to laugh and turn back towards the window, watching the sun begin to set on the horizon. In one hour, I will have to face my wife and stand before her as the failure I have become.

The trip ends, Shaun, and I walk through the terminal carrying our bags making our way to the doors where Amy is waiting to pick us up.

"Steve, I called Carla and she is waiting for me by the parking garage. I figure you will want to be alone with Amy and the kids.

Besides, I need to stop off at the store on the way home." "But, Carla dropped us off and I told you Amy would pick us up." "Do not worry about it and keep your chin up, one day you may be president of Floating for Two."

Turning to each other, we give a warm hug and pat each other on the back. "Your right Shaun, you never know." With that, we leave each other's company and I make my way out of the airport and begin the tense walk towards my awaiting wife.

10

"I love that story; it was a trip I will never forget," Shaun says interrupting me from my story. "I have to go, it's Friday and I'm leaving early today. You have the numbers for last quarter; if you have any questions call me this evening." Shaun rises from his chair extends his hand to Olivia and makes his way to the door. "Oh, by the way, I will be leaving for Phoenix next Tuesday, Aqua Sun and Fun amusement park wants to finalize the distribution details for their order."

"Okay, be careful and call me when you get to Phoenix," I say as he walks out of my office. "What a great friend," Olivia says while making notes on her pad. I respond proudly, "Yes, he gave up a career to help me get this company off the ground and he is an instrumental part of its success."

"I realize that you have other things that you can be doing and I have taken a lot of your time Mr. Woods," Olivia says quietly. Afraid that Olivia cannot not stay for the end of my story I respond, "Not a problem, Olivia." I want to finish my story, if you have the time." I then continue, "As I was saying, I leave the airport and walk towards the car…"

I open the door and peer inside looking at my wife sitting behind the wheel and preparing myself for the worst. As I look at her face, I notice she is smiling at me her eyes and facial expressions tell me that she understands. "I guess you didn't get my message," I say still nervous that she may not know about my meeting in New York.

As we pull away from the airport Amy says, "I listened to it on the answering machine but, while you were gone I realized that having you around and continuing our loving relationship is worth more to me and the kids than all the money in the world." Again, I am amazed and the empty feeling that has plagued my soul these past few days has disappeared. The humming of the car on the pavement lulls me into the rest I had sacrificed these last few days and closing my eyes, I begin to dream.

Once again, I hear the waves crashing and the rumble of thunder growing louder by the minute. Here I am standing on the pier and once more, I am alone. No, I remember, I am not alone, there is a man standing on the rails, leaning over the edge? The young man who has been grasped by the white capped fingers of the waves, pulling him into the sea. I run to the rail at the edge of the pier and yes, I can recall the face. I remember it was me; however, I was not going to let myself become swallowed up and defeated by the unknown. Without thought or warning, I climb up the railing of the pier and as bolts of lightening briefly light up the night sky, I dive into the blackness in an attempt to save the lost soul.

As I fall towards the sea, I lose contact with the man, nothing but a black hole sucking me in faster and faster, no sound of waves, no rumble of thunder, just a black abyss awaiting my arrival. I begin to flail my arms and legs hoping to reach for something or someone, wanting to reach for that little bit of hope I so desperately need to rescue me from certain doom. I think about my family and the great things that lie ahead for us, wondering if I will ever see them again.

There is a crashing sound as I splash into the water gasping for every breath that I can find, not knowing where I am or how to escape this horrible nightmare. The waves bouncing and throwing me around showing no mercy for my well-being as I try to swim for safety. Due to the blackness of the night and the size of the waves, I am not sure which way to go then suddenly, I hear a voice in the distance; it is very faint at first but grows louder with each passing second. The voice seems so familiar, calm and reassuring, even in the rough and unforgiv-ing sea that has consumed my life. "Steven, Steven, Steven, Steven. It's me, Amy!"

It is Amy, swimming around me stabling me from the bounce of the waves reaching, for my hands as if to rescue me from certain doom. "Take my hand Steve, I know the way home." I grab her hand and she pulls my tired exhausted body through the rough waters and onto the shore. We crawl onto the beach and collapse as if we have swam for miles lying face down in the sand still holding onto each other's hands. As I lift my head from the sand and begin to regain my strength, I notice something strange, the sun is now shinning and the cool breeze sways between the tunes of the tropical music that once again play har-mony to my ears.

I am no longer crawling on all fours out of the sea that has taken me in its clutches but, I have risen to my feet and I am standing eye to eye with my wife holding hands and staring at each other as if we have met for the first time. "Amy, I don't know what happened, I was trying to save a man from drowning and at the same time I thought I had lost you in the storm..."

Amy puts her finger to my lips as she had done so many times in the past and says, "Steve, I never left you. During your time on the pier, I knew that you wanted to be alone, to find the answers to questions that you longed to hear. When you thought all hope was lost, I waited for you in the rough seas ahead to show my support and love, a special bond that can never be broken."

I cannot believe what I am hearing, my wife, even though she too has felt as alone and afraid as I, stayed by my side even when I could not see her and for that, I am alive.

Awaking from my sleep I hear the car coming to a screeching halt, I sit up and nervously look over at my wife; she has a smile on her face. "Don't worry Lover; I won't let anything happen to you," she says looking over and putting her hand on my cheek. Little did she realize, I already knew.

11

It has been five years since I began this company and I have never had the Island dream again yet, I cannot help but remember the events that have shaped our lives and how my outlook on life has changed through the passing of events. I take comfort knowing that Amy will always be floating for two in the rough and unforgiving seas that lie before our lives. It is not as if I wish the burden be hers to carry but that seems to be her calling, to be the anchor that holds the family together, regardless of the news or events that may come our way.

The two years following my New York trip, I dedicate to developing my own manufacturing company. Using my knowledge of distribution and international trade, I began to research manufacturing businesses and applied for government loans to sustain my family while developing the company. With the help of Amy and some friends, I have made my dreams a reality. More than anything, I credit my success to a change of mind and heart. I was a man who always thought that appearance and financial stability were the keys to success and happiness; however, I quickly realized that without your family and friends nothing in the world really matters.

One morning during a church service, I glance over my shoulder and notice a little boy in a wheel chair sitting in the aisle next to his family. His father kneeling in the pew with his head down praying, showing more thanks and devotion than I have ever shown. I turn my head back towards my family watching them, knowing that I have been blessed with riches far beyond material goods and large bank accounts.

My road to success has not been an easy journey, nor, would I wish the stresses and failures that I endured on anyone, however, without losing the battles and learning from my mistakes I could have never won the war. I realize now that those failures have played a positive role in my life and they were the inspiration that I needed to continue towards my dreams.

I guess it would be easy to sit at a window and watch the world go by, wondering what could have been and blaming others for my fate but the love I have for my family and the support they have given me has kept me going, working towards the goals that I had set for myself.

A few months ago, I treated my family to a much-needed vacation, the first since the birth of our first son. During the trip, I spent hours relaxing in a beach chair soaking in the beautiful scenery, the wonderful sounds of tropical music and the smell of the sea air watching my wife and our three beautiful sons playing in the white sandy beaches and the gentle surf of the sea.

I begin to wonder if everything is okay at FLOATING FOR TWO INCORPORATED after all, this is the first time since our opening that I have been away for such a long period, other than business travel. As for the men in my dreams on that fateful pier well, they were correct, I do not need them and I have found the courage through my wife and children to make my own dreams come true and paint the most beautiful picture for those I truly love and admire. "No matter," I think to myself, "This is our vacation and I want it to overflow with thoughts of relaxation and family, not of production costs and budgets for pool floats."

Just as I begin to get up to join my wife and children on the beach, a waiter from the hotel rapidly scurries in my direction waving his arms and shouting, "Mr. Woods, Mr. Woods! I have a message for your wife!" As he draws nearer, I notice that he looks a little worn and beads of sweat begin to develop on his brow, as if he has been running, dodging the beach towels and chairs that scatter along the sand. "I wonder what could be so important that this man risks his life to give my wife a message," I think to myself. "Mrs. Woods requested reservations for your family to dine on the pier this evening and I would like to give her the confirmation." He pauses for a moment to catch his breath then continues, "Normally, we are booked months in advance however, today there was a cancellation."

I look at the waiter as he wipes his forehead with an apron that is tied around his waist. "The pier," I think with a nervous sigh. "Sir, I think we will dine in this evening but, thank you anyway," I reply to the man with a nervous tone in my voice. Some moments are for dreams and I have seen my share of piers to last a lifetime. The waiter grumbles words of disgust under his breath and makes his way back to the hotel, navigating his way through the beach chairs and visitors he so desperately tried to avoid while racing to me with the message.

I continue my long decent to the place where water meets sand but along the way, I notice a small flock of geese. "Can it be? No, it can't be." The Gambles were a figment of my imagination, a story on paper. "No, but what if…" I whisper aloud.

I stare more intently at the flock and notice that one of the larger, more dominant geese has left the group and is waddling towards my direction. I continue advancing towards my family but for a short moment, I stop and turn back as if I know this goose is calling to me. We stare at one another but only for a brief moment and I can almost hear him say, "Steve, we did it; we have taken a gamble and survived the stormy sea of life. I wish you well."

At that moment, I turn back towards the sea and race to my family, crying out as if I were the only person on the beach, "Yes Gary, we did it! We did it!"

12

As I finish the interview, telling of the events that have inspired me to live my life and develop my company, I notice Olivia weeping, not loud but just enough to gain my attention. I hand her a box of tissues and sit back into my chair content that my story had a meaning, a purpose.

"I don't know if that was the material you were looking for but you asked about the events that inspired me to develop my product, this company. That's the best that I can offer," I say waiting for her response. "No, it was beautiful; this interview has been the best one for my paper," she says wiping the tears from her eyes as she continues, "I realize now more than ever there is more to developing an idea or operating an organization than what you see on paper or spread sheets."

After a few moments of regaining her composure, Olivia begins to close her notebook and neatly places her things back into her briefcase. "You have a wonderful life and a wonderful family; I hope I can be as lucky as you someday," she says looking at me with wonderment in her eyes.

I look at the clock on my wall and realize that it is nearly three o'clock. I get up from my chair and walk over to Olivia offering a firm handshake and say with a smile on my face, "I'm glad I could be some help to your school paper, if you need anything else, don't hesitate to call."

She stands and looks at my hand that I have offered for her taking and as she moves towards me, I feel her arms wrap around my neck as she provides me with a warm hug. It would have seemed odd, this college student hugging the president of a company just after a meeting; however, I had just given her a small glimpse of my life, my feelings and my thoughts. I guess this was her way of saying thanks.

I walk her to the door and wish her luck in her endeavors, reminding her not to forget the interview, or, the characters that have played such an important part in the success of my business.

As she exits my office, I walk back to my desk and sit down, turning my chair towards the window to view the scenery, once again. A few moments later, I hear Vickie's voice as she enters the room. "What did the two of you talk about Steve?" she asks smiling with curious eyes as she lays down several phone messages from earlier today. "I over heard Olivia on her cell phone talking about a gentleman named Gary, falling into the ocean or something like that…" Vickie continued.

I turn around in my chair grinning from ear to ear and reply, "Vickie when you have a few hours I will explain everything." While saying those words, I grab my briefcase and keys, give her a kiss on the cheek as I pass and advise her that I will be taking the rest of the day off, a personal matter. I notice the puzzled look in her eyes as I head out of the office. I navigate my way through the parking lot and into my car. I begin to drive, a drive that will take me to a place I know all too well, the place where those most dear in my life call home, the place I began my life.

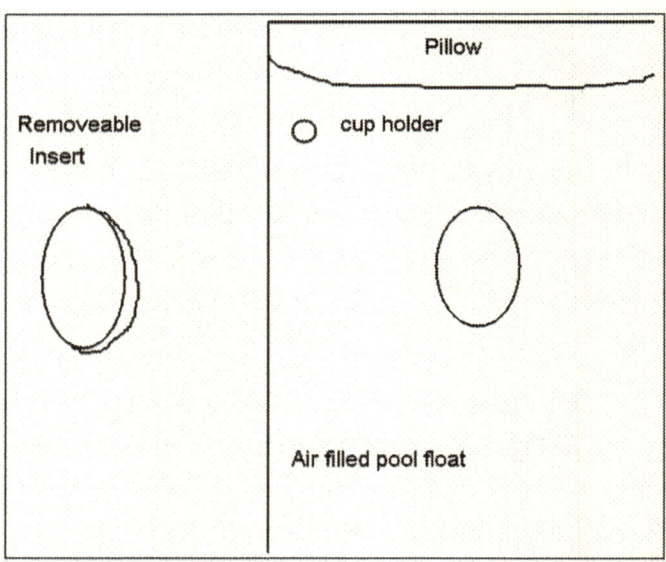

Floating For Two

Pool Float for Expectant Mothers

- Air filled pool float

- Removable Center

- Center can be re-inserted

- Cup Holder

- Pillow for comfort

For Patent information on Floating for Two, contact the U.S. Patent and Trademark Office.

0-595-32432-0